The Tax Bomb in Your Retirement Accounts

How The Roth IRA Can

Help You Avoid It

By: Josh Scandlen, CFP, MS

Contents

Table of Contents

Glossary of Terms

RMDs - *Required Minimum Distributions* - Once you reach 70.5 you must start taking distributions from your tax-deferred retirement accounts...and pay tax on these distributions.

SBP - *Survivor Benefit Plan* - A military retiree may enroll in this plan which allows the spouse to receive 55% of the retirees pension.

NIIT - *Net Investment Income Tax* - This was the tax imposed via the Affordable Care Act which taxes passive income at a higher rate for higher income taxpayers.

OI - *Ordinary Income* - Your marginal tax rate - the worst tax rate you can pay.

LTCG - *Long Term Capital Gain* - A gain on an investment held for over one year and. Taxed much more favorably than STCG.

STCG - *Short Term Capital Gain* - gain on an investment held less than a year, taxed at your marginal rate, or OI.

QDI - *Qualified Dividend Income* - The favorable tax treatment of dividends that qualify, most corporations pay dividends that are taxed as QDI.

MFJ - Married Filing Jointly - Married couples take two standard deductions which can be very beneficial. Don't waste your two standard deductions!

AGI - *Adjusted Gross Income* - The amount found on line 37 of the first page of your 1040 (This line will probably change in 2019). This is BEFORE your standard or itemized deductions.

MAGI - *Modified Adjusted Gross Income* - For Social Security and Medicare calculations your MAGI is your total adjusted gross income and tax-exempt interest income.

PIA - *Primary Insurance Amount* - The full amount you'll receive from Social Security at your FRA.

FRA - *Full Retirement Age* - Born after 1959 your FRA is 67. Born before 1960 your FRA is 66 and maybe some months depending on the exact year you were born.

AIME - *Average Indexed Monthly Earnings* - Your top 35 years of covered earnings (adjusted for inflation) that Social Security uses to calculate your PIA.

TCJA - *Tax Cuts and Job Act of 2017* - substantially raised standard deduction meaning very few retirees will itemize anymore.

Introduction

Do you know how Social Security benefits are taxed? State income taxes? How Medicare premiums are calculated? Ever heard of NIIT? What your RMDs (Required Minimum Distributions) will do to your tax bracket? How about other lump sum distributions? What kind of taxes will your surviving spouse pay? How about the taxes you pass on to your kids?

All of the above will be affected by distributions from your tax-deferred retirement accounts. In this book I'll share with you example after example of how your tax-deferred accounts can greatly increase your overall taxes and even Medicare premiums.

The numbers, once they're laid out for you to see, simply cannot be refuted. Your tax-deferred accounts are like a bomb with a long delay fuze attached to it. The fuze has been lit and at first it creeps slowly along, noticeable only by a few. But, even if not noticed by many, the bomb will go off, causing damage to the ignorant and aware alike.

The Roth is how you douse it.

The Roth is the most powerful financial planning tool ever created to increase your family's wealth. Unfortunately, most people do not understand the significant benefits of the Roth. They see it only as a pay-tax-now vs. pay-tax-later option. The typical analysis as to whether or not one should do a Roth goes something like this:

"I expect my tax bracket to be lower in the future, so it doesn't make sense to do the Roth. Why pay a higher tax rate today to avoid paying tax at a lower rate tomorrow?"

Makes sense, right?

WRONG!

I've seen what happens to clients when IRA distributions account for a larger portion of their income in retirement. Taxes grow and Medicare premiums increase, leaving retirees with less net income even though they have more gross income! Widows, in particular, can find themselves in a very bad financial position with limited options. The Roth, when understood and used correctly, can eliminate much of these higher taxes and premium increases.

Now, in fairness, I'll share four reasons how the Roth can't help you any more than a tax-deferred account can. Not that these four reasons should dissuade you from going full-throttle with the Roth. But I feel it's important to show how the Roth can improve one's financial life and how it can not.

My hope is that after you read this you'll have a much deeper appreciation of the how Roth IRA can enhance your family's wealth--tax-free--for generations. And that you will take advantage of it.

1 - The 50% Tax Increase on IRA Distributions

The single most important thing to understand about the U.S. tax code is the difference between gross income and taxable income.

Let's introduce John and Judy. They have $100,000 in gross income. What do you think their tax bracket is?

IRS Tax Tables for Married Filing Jointly Taxpayers (2018)

	If taxable income is between:
0-$19,050	**10% of Taxable Income**
$19,051-$77,400	**$1,905 + 12% of amount above $19,050**
$77,401-$165,000	**$8,907 + 22% of amount above $77,400**
$165,001-$315,000	**$28,179 + 24% of amount above $165,000**
$315,001-$400,000	**$64,179 + 32% of amount above $315,000**
$400,001-$600,000	**$91,379 + 35% of amount above $400,000**
$600,001 +	**$161,379 + 37% of amount above $600,000**

Table 1

Most people will see a married couple with $100,000 income and think they are in the 22% tax bracket. But that is incorrect.

Taxable Income vs. Gross Income

Your federal tax bracket is actually based on your taxable income not your gross income. Taxable income is the net amount you have after you take the various deductions and/or exemptions that are available.

So, let's assume John and Judy do not itemize their taxes. The only deduction they have is the standard deduction.

Under the new tax bill, (TCJA 2017), tax payers under 65 years old can take $12,000 in standard deductions. Taxpayers 65 and older have a standard deduction of $13,300. Assuming John and Judy are both over 65, they would subtract $26,600 from their $100,000 of gross income. Their taxable income would then be $73,400, which puts them in the 12% bracket. They will pay $8,426 in federal income tax.

But what happens if they add $10,000 by taking a distribution from a Traditional IRA? Now their taxable income is $83,400 which puts them in the 22% tax bracket. Their tax is $10,227, an increase of around $1,800.

Put another way, that $10,000 distribution accounted for 9.1% of their total income yet 17.6% of their total tax bill.

Look at the table below and you can see how the $10,000 IRA distribution affected John and Judy's taxes.

	No IRA Distribution	$10,000 IRA Distribution
Income	$100,000	$100,000
IRA Distributions	$0	$10,000
Adjusted Gross Income	$100,000	$110,000
Standard Deductions	$26,600	$26,600
Taxable Income	$73,400	$83,400
Tax Due	$8,426	$10,227

Table 2

Most taxpayers understand that tax rates go up as income increases. What gets overlooked is that the actual percentage of that increase is huge. In John and Judy's case, it was a 50% increase!

How? Because that $10,000 distribution cost them $1,801 in additional tax, meaning their effective tax rate on that distribution was 18.01%. If they have remained in the 12% bracket their tax would have been $1,200.

What would happen if that $10,000 IRA distribution came from a Roth though?

	$10,000 Roth Distribution
Income	$100,000
Roth IRA Distributions	$10,000
Adjusted Gross Income	$100,000
Standard Deductions	-$26,600
Taxable Income	$73,400
Tax Due	$8,426

Table 3

11

Roth distributions are tax free so that $10,000 will not be included in any taxable calculation. They have that extra $10,000 to spend. They just don't pay tax on it.

Now, you might argue, "Yes, Josh, your numbers are sound but they received a deduction on the money going into the IRA to begin with. You would have to compare the tax they pay now to the savings they had before."

This is correct. We certainly need to look at the tax savings of the IRA deduction against the tax free withdrawals of the Roth.

However, my experience is that many working taxpayers don't have near the taxable income they think they do given varying tax deductions and credits: mortgage interest, credits for children, real estate tax, etc. In fact, let me ask you, do you know what the number on line 47 of your own 1040 is? That is your total tax. How much of that tax was reduced by your itemized deductions?

Unfortunately, most taxpayers actually retire into higher tax brackets because their Required Minimum Distributions put them there and they no longer have any itemized deductions, which is exactly what happened to John and Judy. At that point, there is not much they can do other than pay the tax. But keep on reading and you'll see the many other overlooked benefits of the Roth.

2 - Don't Get Sucked into the Widow's Tax Trap

If you are a married filing jointly (MFJ) taxpayer you will not be one indefinitely. At some point, you or your spouse will be a single taxpayer and your tax situation will change dramatically.

Let's go back to John and Judy. Their income is $100,000 which consists of John's military pension and IRA distributions. Their tax situation looks like this:

John and Judy's Income ($100,000 Gross)	
IRA distribution	$45,000
Pension	$55,000
Adjusted Gross	$100,000
Standard Deductions	-$26,600
Taxable Income	$73,400
Tax Due	$8,426

Table 4

Now, let's say John dies. Thankfully, he filed for a 55% Survivor Benefit Pension (SBP) when he separated from the military which allows Judy to receive a pension benefit of $30,250. However, that's not enough for Judy to live on. She feels she needs a gross income of $75,000 to maintain her lifestyle. So, the rest of her income will come from IRA distributions. *(In case you are wondering about Social Security, we'll get into that later. That's where it really gets fun!)*

This is what the line items will look like when she goes to file her taxes:

Judy's Income ($75,000 Gross)	
Pension	$30,250
IRA Distribution	$44,750
Adjusted Gross	$75,000
Standard Deductions	-$13,300
Taxable Income	$61,700
Tax Due	$9,513

Table 5

Anything jump out at you?

Judy has 33% less income yet pays 13% more in federal tax!

How can this be?

On the next page you will see the tax tables for a single taxpayer in 2018. Notice that a single taxpayer is in the 22% bracket when taxable income exceeds $38,700. A married couple must have income above $77,400 before they are in the 22% bracket. The married couple also gets two standard deductions whereas a single taxpayer only gets one.

If taxable income is between:	Tax
0-$9,525	10% of taxable income
$9,525-$38,700	$953 + 12% of amount above $9,525
$38,701-$82,500	$4,453 + 22% of amount above $38,700
$82,501 - $157,500	$14,089 + 24% of amount above $82,500
$157,501 - $200,000	$32,089 + 32% of amount above $157,500
$200,001 - $500,000	$45,689 + 35% of amount above $200,000
$500,001 +	$150,689 + 37% of amount above $500,000

Table 6

Higher Tax Rate + Less Standard Deduction = MUCH MORE TAX

And there you have the Widow's Tax Trap; Less income and more tax. Now, if Judy had Roth IRA distributions instead of Traditional IRA her tax bill would have only been $1,844!

Judy's Income with Roth Distribution ($75,000 Gross)	
Pension	$30,250
Roth IRA Distribution	$44,750
Adjusted Gross	$30,250
Standard Deductions	-$13,300
Taxable Income	$16,950
Tax Due	$1,844

Table 7

3 - Do This and You Won't Pay Tax on Your Social Security Benefits

In 1983, and again in 1993, provisions were made to the tax code to allow for the taxation of Social Security benefits. If your income was above a certain provision some of your benefits were taxed. Thus the term "provisional income" came to describe how much of your Social Security benefits are taxed.

Oddly, go to SSA.gov and type "provisional income" into the search button and see what you come up with; Nothing.

Go to IRS.gov and type in "provisional income". Again, nothing.

Now, don't get me wrong, both of these sites have tons of information on how benefits are taxed.
Here's the IRS for example:

- *a quick way to find out if a taxpayer must pay taxes on their Social Security benefits: Add one-half of the Social Security income to all other income, including tax-exempt interest. Then compare that amount to the base amount for their filing status. If the total is more than the base amount, some of their benefits may be taxable.*
- ***Base Amounts.*** *The three base amounts are:*
  - *$25,000 – if taxpayers are single, head of household, qualifying widow or widower with a dependent child or married filing separately and lived apart from their spouse for all of 2018*
  - *$32,000 – if they are married filing jointly*

- $0 – *if they are married filing separately and lived with their spouse at any time during the year*

Clear as mud, no?

This complexity is why the vast majority of Americans have no clue how their Social Security benefits are taxed, to include most financial advisors. This is unfortunate given how many Americans rely heavily on their Social Security in retirement.

Understanding Provisional Income

Kiplinger's magazine is a good source for Social Security information. They write: "Your provisional income is your adjusted gross income, not counting Social Security benefits, *plus nontaxable interest* and half of your Social Security benefits"(emphasis mine).

To illustrate how this works let's bring back John and Judy. We'll say they have $100k of total income which consists of $45k in Social Security, $40k of pension and IRA distributions and $15k of tax-exempt municipal bond interest.

To calculate their provisional income, we simply add half of their Social Security benefits to their pension and IRA distributions. As the the next table shows they have $77,500 in provisional income.

John and Judy's Provisional Income	
Half of Social Security	$22,500
Pension and IRA Income	$40,000
Tax Exempt Interest	$15,000
Total Provisional Income	**$77,500**

Table 8

Now we need to find out how much of John and Judy's Social Security benefits will be taxable. We use the formula provided by from IRS.gov:

Tax Filing Status	Provisional Income	Social Security Taxation
Single or head of household	Less than $25,000	0%
	$25,000 - $34,000	Up to 50%
	More than $34,000	Up to 85%
Joint filers	Less than $32,000	0%
	$32,000 - $44,000	Up to 50%
	More than $44,000	Up to 85%

(Source:
https://www.fool.com/knowledge-center/how-to-calculate-provisional-income.aspx)

$77,500 in Provisional Income		
Income Range	**% Taxable**	**Taxable**
$32,000	0	0
$12,000	50%	$6,000
$33,500	85%	$28,475
Taxable SS		**$34,475**

Table 9

And we find that $34,475, or 77% of John and Judy's Social Security benefit, will be subject to income tax.

Finally, we need to calculate their taxable income and the tax they'll owe. We do this by adding their taxable Social Security benefit to their other income sources (not including the $15k in municipal bond interest this time.)

$100,000 Total Income	
Taxable Social Security	$34,475
IRA Distribution	$40,000
Adjusted Gross	$74,475
Standard Deductions	-$26,600
Taxable Income	$47,875
Tax Due	**$5,364**

Table 10

As you can see from the table above, with taxable income of $47,875 their federal tax bill is $5,364.

How a Roth Changes Things

Now let's change things around a bit. John and Judy still have
$100,000 income but now it consists solely of Social Security
and Roth IRA distributions.

John and Judy's Income Sources	
John's Social Security	$30,000
Judy's Social Security	$15,000
Roth IRA Distributions	$55,000
Total Income	**$100,000**

Table 11

Want to guess what their income tax is now? Nothing. Why?
Because, going back to Kiplinger's, if you are married filing
jointly and your provisional income is "less than $32,000 you
won't owe taxes on your benefit."

In John and Judy's case, their provisional income is only
$22,500. $22,500 < $32,000 thus no tax due on their Social
Security benefit. Of course, Roth distributions are tax free as
well. $100,000 income and not one penny in federal tax!

John and Judy's Provisional Income with Roth Distributions	
Total Social Security Benefit	$45,000
Half of Social Security Benefit	$22,500
All other Income	$0
Tax Exempt Interest	$0
Total Provisional Income	$22,500

Table 12

Try this one for yourself:

You are married and your provisional income is $65,000. You have $27,000 in Social Security benefits.

Quiz: Can you calculate how much of Social Security will be taxed in the example?

Provisional Income:	$65,000	Taxable Rate	Taxable Amount
Less than $32,000	?	0%	$0
$32,000 - $44,000	?	50%	$0
More than $44,000	?	85%	$0
Total Social Security Subject To Tax			?
85% of Social Security Benefit:			?
Use Lessor of the two above amounts:			?

Table 13

Remember, if your provisional income is more than $44,000 we know that at least $6,000 will be subject to tax. 85% of any amount above $44,000 will also be subject to tax.

Add the 50% amount ($6,000) to the 85% amount ($17,850) and we come up with a taxable Social Security benefit of $23,850.

Finally, we find the lesser of the $23,850 or 85% of the total Social Security benefit which in this example is $27,000. 85% of $27,000 is $22,950. That is the amount of Social Security subject to tax.

Provisional Income of:	$65,000	Taxable Rate	Taxable Amount
Less than $32,000	$32,000	0%	$0
$32,000 - $44,000	$12,000	50%	$4,500
More than $34,000	$21,000	85%	$26,350
Total			$30,850
85% of Social Security Benefit:			$22,950
Use Lessor of the two above amounts:			$22,950

Table 14

To figure your taxable income you just add that $22,950 to your other taxable income sources, be they earned income, passive income, IRA distributions, pensions etc. Roth distributions are not included. Which means the only way to have tax free Social Security benefits is to have Roth IRA distributions.

4 - How One Widow Paid $9,623 in Tax While Another Widow Paid $0

As we discussed in the previous chapter, if a married couple's provisional income is less than $32k they pay no tax on their Social Security benefits. However, for a single taxpayer, if provisional income is greater than $34k then up to 85% of his/her Social Security benefit will be subject to tax.

Let's say you are a single taxpayer and have a $30,000 distribution from a Traditional IRA in addition to your $30,000 of Social Security benefits. In this case your provisional income is $45,000. You will pay tax on your Social Security Benefits.

Remember: Provisional Income is half your Social Security benefit plus __any__ other income you receive (Roth distributions excluded).

Now say that $30,000 IRA distribution came from a Roth. In this case your provisional income is only $15,000 because Roth IRAs are not included in the calculations. So, you pay NO TAX!

Look at the chart below to see how this breaks down for Judy and Jane.

Income Sources:	Judy	Jane
Social Security	$30k	$30k
IRA Distributions	$30k	0
Roth Distributions	0	$30k
Total Income	**$60k**	**$60k**

Table 15

They each have $60,000 of income, $30,000 from Social Security and $30,000 from IRAs. Judy's IRA income is from a Traditional but Jane's is from a Roth.

Now let's see what this looks like when it comes to the taxes they pay.

	Judy	Jane
Taxable IRA Distributions	$30,000	0
Taxable Social Security	$13,850	0
Adjusted Gross Income	$43,850	0
Standard Deduction	-$13,300	-$13,300
Taxable Income	$30,550	0
Tax Due	**$3,476**	**0**

Table 16

By having a Traditional IRA, Judy has to pay $3,476 in tax. Jane pays nothing. Over the course of 10 years Judy will pay nearly $35,000 more in federal income tax than Jane. Since most state income taxes are based on taxable income calculated for a federal return, the figure may be even higher.

Just think about what you could do with an extra $3,476 each year. That could be the premiums for your Long Term Care

Insurance policy or it could be your car payment, Medicare premiums, etc.

But Wait There's More!

Ever since John died, Judy has wanted to take her daughter on a month-long cruise vacation. "No time like the present," she said. So, she takes an IRA distribution of $50k to pay for the cruise. Much fun was had.

But smiles turn to frowns when Judy gets a call from her tax guy the following year. She owes almost $10,000 in federal income taxes! Nearly $7,000 more than the year before even though she only increased her gross income by $20,000.

Her income went up by $20k, a 33% increase. But her taxes went up nearly $7k, a 250% increase!

How does this happen? Well let's break it down, step by step.

STEP 1: Determine Total Income

Judy's Total Income	
Income Sources:	**Judy**
Social Security	$30,000
Traditional IRA Distributions	$50,000
Total Income	**$80,000**

Table 17

STEP 2: Determine Judy's Provisional Income

Judy's Provisional Income	
Half of Social Security Benefit	$15,000
ALL other income	$50,000
Tax Exempt Interest	$0
Total Provisional Income	**$65,000**

Table 18

STEP 3: Determine Taxable Social Security

Judy's Provisional Income	$65,000	Taxable Rate	Taxable Amount
Less than $25,000	$25,000	0%	$0
$25,000 - $34,000	$9,000	50%	$4,500
More than $34,000	$31,000	85%	$25,075
Total Social Security Subject to Tax:			$29,575
85% of Social Security Benefit:			$25,500
Use Lesser of the two above amounts:			$25,500

Table 19

STEP 4: Determine Judy's tax

How Judy's Taxes Are Determined	
Taxable Distributions	$50,000
Taxable Social Security	$25,500
Adjusted Gross Income	$75,500
Standard Deduction	$13,300
Taxable Income	$62,200
Tax	**$9,623**

Table 20

Judy is stunned to learn that by taking out $20,000 more from her IRA she raised her taxes by $6,146, which is an effective 32% rate.

I can hear you asking, "Wait a second! She's in the 22% tax bracket. How is her effective tax on this distribution 32%? This seems fishy!"

Indeed, it IS fishy! But it is reality.

She is being taxed twice on the same income. Those IRA distributions are subject to income tax but it also made more of her Social Security benefits taxed as well. When Judy only had a $30,000 IRA distribution just $13,850 of her Social Security benefit was taxable.

But now with the $50,000 IRA distribution, her taxable Social Security benefit jumped to to $25,500. Her total total taxable income more than doubled from $30,550 last year to $63,500. A

33% increase in gross income caused a 100% increase in taxable income. A better example of double taxation you won't find.

How the Roth Saves the Day...Once Again

Now, let's look at Jane. She also increased her income by $50,000 to take her daughter on that same 30-day cruise. But Jane has a Roth IRA, not a Traditional.

What happened to her taxes??? Nothing. She NETS $80,000 and she still pays no tax. Her provisional income is still under the threshold for her Social Security benefit to remain tax free. No tax on Social Security, no tax on Roth = no tax due.

I know there are disbelievers among you. So, follow the steps below to see exactly why Jane pays no tax.

Step 1: Determine Total Income

Jane's Total Income	
Income Sources:	**Jane**
Social Security	$30,000
Roth IRA Distributions	$50,000
Total Income:	**$80,000**

Table 21

Step 2: Determine Provisional Income

Jane's Provisional Income	
Half of Social Security Benefit	$15,000
ALL other income	$0
Tax-Exempt Interest	$0
Total Provisional Income	**$15,000**

Table 22

STEP 3: Determine Taxable Social Security

Jane's Provisional Income	$15,000	Taxable Rate	Taxable Amount
Less than $25,000	$15,000	0%	$0
$25,000 - $34,000	$0	50%	$0
More than $34,000	$0	85%	<u>$0</u>
Total Social Security Subject to Tax			$0
85% of Social Security Benefit:			$25,500
Use Lesser of the two above amounts:			$0

Table 23

STEP 4: Determine Tax

How Jane's Taxes Are Determined	
Taxable Distributions	$0
Taxable Social Security	$0
Adjusted Gross Income	$0
Standard Deduction	$13,300
Taxable Income	$0
Tax	**$0**

Table 24

Jane pays nothing on $80,000 of income. Judy pays almost $10,000 in federal income taxes on the same income. Who would you rather be?

5 - The Easy Way to Avoid Doubling, Even Tripling, Your Medicare Premiums

With a Roth there are NO required minimum distributions (RMDs). This means you can allow your Roth to grow for as long as you are breathing without ever having to take any money out.

A traditional IRA, 401k, 403B or TSP all require at age 70½ you begin taking a percentage out of the account in order to pay tax on it. What if you don't need the money? Doesn't matter. The IRS needs it more and they will get it starting when you turn 70.½.

Let's say you are 70 years old and have $100,000 in your traditional IRA. Your RMD will be $3,649.63.

How did I get that? Just take your account balance from the end of the previous year, find your age at the end of this year on the IRS table below and divide that corresponding number into your account balance.

RMD Table For Your Own IRA

This also covers an IRA inherited from a spouse

Age	Divisor	Age	Divisor
70	27.4	86	14.1
71	26.5	87	13.4
72	25.6	88	12.7
73	24.7	89	12.0
74	23.8	90	11.4
75	22.9	91	10.8
76	22.0	92	10.2
77	21.2	93	9.6
78	20.3	94	9.1
79	19.5	95	8.6
80	18.7	96	8.1
81	17.9	97	7.6
82	17.1	98	7.1
83	16.3	99	6.7
84	15.5	100	6.3
85	14.8		

source: IRS Pub 590

Now, I can hear some saying "Josh, paying tax on $3,649.63 is no big deal. I'm in the 12% bracket so it will only cost me around $400 in taxes."

I agree. The first few years of RMDs are so small you probably won't even notice the tax hit. In fact, your account will probably grow *more* than your required distributions. How about when you get older though? At 82, say you still have $100,000 in your account, your RMD will have increased 60% to $5,847.95.

These RMDs begin to add up when it comes to the taxes you pay on your Social Security as well and, unbeknownst to most, your Medicare Part B and D premiums too!

How Medicare Premiums Double...or Worse!

Medicare premiums are means-tested which means the higher your income the more your premiums will be. We aren't talking chump change here either, folks. A single taxpayer with a Modified Adjusted Gross Income (MAGI) of less than $85,000, pays $134 in monthly Medicare Part B premiums and $34 in Part D premiums But once that taxpayer goes above $107,000 in MAGI, her monthly premiums double from $168 to $335!

MAGI = <u>All</u> Income Before Deductions (excluding Roth)

The higher the MAGI, the larger the premium. The maximum premium for Medicare is $504.80 per beneficiary, which is an increase of nearly 400% from the lowest premium!

Higher RMDs = higher taxable income = much higher Medicare premiums.

6 - Tax Free Wealth for a "Non-Working" Spouse

Let's say you are the breadwinner and your spouse is a stay home mom or dad.

Due to all the contributions to your retirement plan at work your side of the balance sheet is growing significantly more than your spouse's. You are concerned about "equalization of estates". (Equalization of estates is an old estate planning term when there was more concern with estate tax. The estate tax issue is a non-starter for most nowadays but there is something to be said for both spouses having ownership in *something*.)

What you should do is plop down $5,500 in January in your Spouse's Roth IRA. Doesn't matter if he or she isn't "working" for an income. Only matters that you are.

Do this every year and you'll be surprised at how quickly the account can grow. Have I mentioned that Roth's grow TAX-FREE too???

7 - This Is The PERFECT Retirement Plan

With a Roth *you* determine when you want to pay the taxes for what you put into the account. This is a benefit of the Roth that way too often gets overlooked.

Remember, anything contributed to a Roth is with after-tax money. If you choose the Roth, you pay tax now. If you choose the Traditional you pay tax later. It's up to you when you want to pay the tax.

You can also convert all or a portion of your Traditional IRA/401k/403B/TSP to a Roth. A conversion is simply moving money from a tax-deferred account to a Roth. For instance, if you were to convert $50,000 from your Traditional IRA to a Roth, that $50,000 will be taxable as ordinary income (OI) in the year in which you did it. There is no escaping that. You will pay tax on that converted amount. But again, you choose when.

Let's play out a scenario to see how this may work for you. Sarah and Dan just retired. As a marketing executive Sarah was making good money, $150,000 a year with a $50,000 annual bonus. Dan was also making a decent income as a sales consultant, $75,000 a year. Between them they had $275,000 a year in gross income.

Because their kids were no longer at home and the mortgage was paid off the only deductions they had were deferring as much income as possible to their 401k plans. Last year they were both able to defer the maximum of $22,000.

Those deferrals, plus their two standard deductions, reduced their gross income by $68,000 (see table below). Their taxable income then was $207,000, putting them right in the middle of the 24% bracket.

Calculate Gross and Taxable Income with 401k Deferrals	
Earned Income	$225,000
Bonus	$50,000
Gross Income	$275,000
401k deferrals	$44,000
Standard Deductions	$24,000
Taxable income	**$207,000**

Table 25

As the next table shows, Sarah and Dan pay nearly $40,000 in federal income tax on a gross income of $275,000 for an effective rate of 13.8%. Not too bad, eh?

Calculate Sarah and Dan's Tax With 401k Deferrals		
Marginal Tax Rates	**Taxable Income**	**Tax**
10%	$19,050	$1,905
12%	$58,350	$7,002
22%	$87,600	$19,272
24%	$42,000	$10,080
Total Tax		$38,259
Effective Tax Rate	**13.80%**	

Table 26

By maximizing their deferrals they were able to reduce their taxable income by 16%, which saved them $10,000 in taxes.

The next table shows their taxes when they do the Roth 401k and don't get immediate tax deferrals.

Calculate Gross and Taxable Income Roth 401k	
Earned Income	$225,000
Bonus	$50,000
Gross Income	$275,000
Standard Deductions	$24,000
Taxable income	**$251,000**

Table 27

You can see their taxable income increased to $251k and their taxes owed increased as well, by $10,500.

Calculate Sarah and Dan's Tax No 401k Deferrals		
Marginal Tax Rates	Taxable Income	Tax
10%	$19,050	$1,905
12%	$58,350	$7,002
22%	$87,600	$19,272
24%	$86,000	$20,640
Total Tax		**$48,819**
Effective Tax Rate	**17.75%**	

Table 28

But remember, there is a HUGE difference between *deferring* income, 401k contributions, and *negating* taxable income, standard deductions. Deferring income simply means you don't pay tax on that income now but you will at some point.

Ages 62-70 are the Golden Years of Tax Planning

Fast forward a few years and we see that both Sarah and Dan have just retired. Sarah is 62 and Dan 66. They are not taking Social Security yet just living off the savings they were able to squirrel away.

They have no mortgage and they figure they spend about $50,000 a year total, on everything, vacations, bills, helping the kids out occasionally, etc.

Should They Take Social Security Now?

They have accumulated $300k in their 401ks and rolled those accounts to IRAs. They also have $150k in savings accounts. They wonder if they should start taking Social Security.

NO! Absolutely not!

Given they have no income other than minimal interest they're making on their bank account they are paying NO TAX. They will continue to pay NO TAX until they reach 70.5 when RMDs kick in. They should take advantage of their $0 tax and start moving money over to a Roth, now! Any income they receive up to $25,300 is TAX FREE! ($12,000 is the Standard Deduction in 2018 for Sarah and $13,300 for Dan).

When Your Tax Rates are Low, Convert to Roths!

Let's say I am able to convince them to convert $50,000 this year. That $50,000 *will* be taxable as ordinary income. But with their $25,300 of standard deductions kicking in and the fact they have no other income their taxable income will be all of $24,700. They'll pay only $2,583 in taxes this year.

$2,583 in tax today is a tiny price to pay for all the benefits of the Roth IRA. Heck, I'd even advocate they convert a full $100,000. With a $100,000 conversion their total tax will be $8,655. But that $100,000 plus any growth will NEVER SUBJECT TO TAXATION AGAIN!

A Beautiful Retirement Plan

If they convert $100,000 in year 1, $100,000 in year 2 and the rest in year 3, they'll have moved all their money from their to-be-taxed accounts to never-taxed-again accounts.

In year 4, when they have exhausted their cash savings, then they both take Social Security. Dan will get his as a 69-year-old, meaning he'll have nearly maximized his Delayed Earnings Credits (DEC) and will enjoy a significant bump in his benefit.

Say Dan averaged $75,000 a year over his career. His Averaged Indexed Monthly Earnings (AIME) will be $6,250. This means his Primary Insurance Amount (PIA) will be $2,519 at his Full Retirement Age (FRA). If he waits to file for Social Security at 69 his Social Security benefit will be $3173 a month because of the three years of Delayed Earnings Credits. (I won't get into Social Security here, I have lots of other resources on my youtube channel at www.youtube.com/heritagewealthplanning).

If Sarah made the maximum under the Social Security rules at her FRA her benefit would be around $2800 a month. But because she is going to file at 65, a year before her FRA, her benefit will be reduced to $2,600 a month.

Following this strategy, Dan and Sarah will receive nearly $70,000 a year in Social Security benefits, which will meet all their income needs and it will be TAX FREE.

If they need to dip into their Roth IRAs to augment their Social Security income they can do so and will still pay no tax. It's a beautiful thing to behold. Their primary source of income is

Social Security which will be tax free augmented by tax-free Roth IRA distributions.

Dan and Sarah have another 20-25 years ahead of them and they will NEVER pay income tax again. Let that sink in. Can that work for you too? Absolutely!

Roth IRA + Social Security = An Amazing Benefit of the Tax Code

The beauty of this retirement cannot be overstated. Yet, very few people take advantage. Why? They've been taught, incorrectly, to defer taxes as long as possible. I take issue with this philosophy. If you can pay a small amount of tax today to avoid huge taxes in the future, you absolutely should.

8 - How to Pay No Tax on Dividends and Capital Gains

If you are married filing jointly with taxable income of $77,400 or less, you are in the 12% tax bracket. However, add $1 more and you are in the 22% bracket. See how that works? $77,400 = 12% bracket. $77,401 = 22% bracket.

This is how marginal rates work: the more income you receive the higher the tax rate on that <u>additional income</u> will be. The tax you paid on your previous income doesn't change though. You only pay higher taxes on the amount that puts you into the next bracket.

How Qualified Dividends and Long-Term Gains Are Taxed

Now, let's say you have total income of $70,000 which consists of $60,000 of work income and $10,000 in the form of Qualified Dividend Income (QDI) and Long Term Capital Gains (LTCG). But you need $80,000 to maintain your lifestyle. So you take a $10,000 distribution from your IRA. That puts you in the 22% tax bracket.

The following April you go visit your tax guy to file your taxes. Your tax guy gives you what you initially thought to be a pleasant surprise. He says that you only have to pay 15% on the $10,000 you received as dividends and capital gains even though you are in the 22% tax bracket. This is good news, right?

Unfortunately, the reason you're in the 22% bracket to begin with is the IRA distribution put you there. Now, you owe over $3,000 in taxes. This is bad.

You wise up and use a different strategy for the following year. You still need $80,000 to get by. You're still only making $70,000 from work and dividends. To make up the difference this year you take a distribution from your Roth IRA, not your Traditional.

Now, when you go back to your tax guy you really do get a pleasant surprise: you pay $3,000 less in taxes! "Wait a second. How can this be?" You ask.

Your tax guy explains. "Your IRA distribution last year not only increased your marginal tax rate to 22% but it also made your dividends and capital gains taxable as well. That $10,000 IRA distribution cost you $1,500 in income tax *plus* $1,500 in taxes on your dividends and capital gains. A double-whammy if ever there was one!

"Because your Roth distribution is tax free you remain in the 12% bracket. Taxpayers who are in the 10% or 12% brackets do not pay tax on their qualified dividends or long term capital gains. So, not only do you not pay taxes on your Roth, you don't pay taxes on your other investment income either!"

Isn't the Roth beautiful?

Taxpayers in the 10% or 12% Brackets Pay ZERO on QDI and LTCG

Many people believe they are saving on taxes with their IRA because they are deferring the tax until later. This is true for some taxpayers, especially those currently in a high tax bracket. Deferring a high tax now until later when they may be in a lower bracket is smart planning.

But what about taxpayers in the 10%, 12% or 22% brackets? Are they actually saving taxes by deferring though? I don't think so.

Some analysis, of course, would need to go into your specific situation but don't simply fall for the fallacy that deferring income saves taxes. It most certainly may not. In fact, as the example above shows, it could actually lead you to pay more in tax, maybe even a lot more.

To close this chapter, please remember you want to reduce ordinary income taxed investments, like bonds and Traditional IRAs, and increase your tax favorable investments, such as Roth IRAs, qualified dividends and long-term capital gains. If you can get your income to be from Social Security, Roth distributions, qualified dividends and long-term capital gains, you are going to be in a very good place from a tax perspective.

9 - No Tax = MORE GROWTH

Traditional IRA growth is stunted by tax

The Roth has no RMDs which means it can grow for as long as you and your spouse live. You cannot get the same growth potential in a Traditional IRA where you are mandated to take distributions each year.

Think about it like this. You and your spouse are both 68 years old. What is better to have, a $100,000 tax-deferred account or a $75,000 tax-free account?

The answer is the tax-free account. Seems counterintuitive doesn't it? $75,000 is significantly less money than $100,000 after all. But the *entirety* of that $75,000 account is yours. And you never have to touch it unless you want.

That $100,000 has a huge lien on it called the IRS. Slowly at first, but in a few short years RMDs will increase until the account is nearly depleted.

One could argue that you could take the RMDs from the tax-deferred account and invest them in a side account. But you still paid tax on the RMDs as ordinary income. Secondly, if your side account has its own distributions you could pay tax there too. Even if you're in the 10% or 12% brackets and don't pay tax on capital gains or qualified dividends you still pay ordinary income tax on interest. That interest can also move you into a higher tax bracket, potentially causing your dividends and capital gains to be taxed too.

Because there are no RMD requirements the Roth can pass from one spouse to another without ever being touched. We're talking potential for decades of tax-free growth.

When non-spouses inherit a Roth, they do have RMDs. But even those RMDs are tax free. The Roth simply can't be topped when it comes to generational tax-free growth.

10 - How to Leave a Large Tax-Free Inheritance Without Life Insurance

It is my opinion that the Roth IRA is the most effective *and* underutilized method of transferring wealth to future generations.

Now, I can hear all the life insurance agents screaming, "Roth is NOT preferable to life insurance!" To my life insurance friends, in some ways I agree. There is no other method where one could create an *instant* estate as quickly as life insurance.

Only life insurance can create an instant estate

For instance, say you're 45 years old, making good money and in good health. Your net worth consists of the equity in your home and $250k in retirement savings.

One day you get hit by a bus and die. Your spouse will inherit your equity in the home plus your $250k in retirement savings (assuming the house was jointly owned and he/she was beneficiary on the retirement account).

While that's a decent amount of wealth, it isn't generational wealth by any stretch. And, of course, at some point your spouse will be forced to pay taxes on the retirement account, thus reducing its value.

However, for pennies on the dollar you could buy a $2 million-dollar life insurance policy. But there's a couple problems with this scenario.

The most obvious, of course, is that you had to *die* for that sizeable estate to be created. Maybe not a big deal if you're in your late 80s and have major health issues but for a 45-year-old with kids, you probably want to avoid that.

The second issue is that you have to pay for the life insurance premiums until you die and who knows when that will be? So, your premium payments could continue for many, many years to come.

The *vast* majority of life insurance policies never actually pay out. Most people stop paying the premiums well before they die. But what if you commit to paying premiums in order to have a policy pay out at your death? Well, you still have to get underwritten for the policy. The older you are the more difficult to get approved and the more expensive the insurance will be.

When you're young and in good health life insurance is easy to get and cheap too. But while a policy on a 45-year-old woman who is in good health will not be very expensive, is multi-generational wealth creation something that is of foremost importance to her if she is a divorced, working mother with children to raise, college costs to consider and her own retirement to save for?

I highly suspect not. So, while I do love life insurance and believe everyone should get a term policy when they're young it is not superior to a Roth for multi-generational wealth planning.

Imagine if the Roth IRA existed in 1972. You were in sales, going door to door selling encyclopedias. Your efforts paid off when you stumbled onto a neighborhood with a large number of buyers who really liked the idea of having all that information at their fingertips. You had a great year in 1972. Your best ever, in fact. So, you decided to invest $5,000 of your after-tax commissions into this account called a Roth IRA.

Unfortunately, in the first two years after you made the investment, the markets fell 14% in 1973 and 26% in 1974. Your $5,000 fell to $3,186 by the start of 1975. You had discipline, though, and just let it sit there. "Easy come, easy go," you said to yourself.

Then the magic of compounding interest began to work. Even with the massive crash of 1973 and 1974 you averaged 10% a year over the next three decades.

Since this account was a Roth IRA there were never any Required Minimum Distributions. And you never touched the money. Just let it grow.

Unfortunately, in 2006 you got hit by a bus and went to your Greater Reward. But before you left this earth, with your last breath, you asked your wife "please don't touch that Roth IRA we started back in '72. Just let it sit there for the kids."

October 2007 came around and times got scary with investments. By March 2009 the inheritance was cut in half! Your wife thought that maybe it was time to get out of the market to protect what was left.

After some thought, though, she just said, "well, it's gone down so far, might as just let it ride. After all, we only started with $5000." And she did just that.

In January of 2018 your wife got hit by that same daggum bus and joined you in Paradise. But before she took her last breath she looked at the Roth statement one last time. She was amazed. That $5,000 you put into the Roth back in 1972 was now worth $364,000, tax free.

Hundreds of thousands of tax-free dollars were created from a tiny $5,000 investment. Farfetched? Nope. These are actual real-world numbers, starting during the huge market crash of 1973 and 1974.

This multi-generational wealth planning is within your grasp, if you are disciplined enough.

11 - Pay 10% Now or 35% Later?

After John died, Judy lived rather frugally, as do most retirees. So, when she died she still had $200,000 in her IRA. She left 50% each to her two children, Jimmy and Jenny.

Jimmy is a married Radiologist making $500k a year. Jenny is a divorced gas station attendant making $35k a year and heavily in debt.

Jimmy has no cash flow needs so he rolls the $100,000 Judy left him into an inherited IRA. He still needs to take annual required minimum distributions. But while those distributions won't be much initially because he is only 50 years old they will grow each year. Unfortunately for him, as long as he's making the same income he's going to lose 35%, or more, to federal income taxes.

Unlike Jimmy, Jenny is in desperate need of cash. Creditors are calling and she is late on rent. She takes a lump sum distribution of the entire $100,000 which put her gross income for the year at $135,000. Her total tax will be around $23,800 once she takes the distribution, which means she is going to lose nearly 25% of the amount she inherited! Ultimately, a third of John and Judy's savings will be lost to taxes.

Tax-Free Inheritance or Taxable?

Regardless if you're a high-income earner like Jimmy who doesn't need the cash, or a low income earner like Jenny who desperately does, wouldn't you rather receive the inheritance tax free so you could keep all of the proceeds?

If John and Judy had left their children Roth IRAs every single penny would have gone to them and none to the IRS. All that was required was for the to have done a bit of tax planning while they were alive.

Be advised, there is no getting around paying tax. Someone is going to pay some tax. But with proper planning, John and Judy may have been able to pay tax at 10% which would have allowed the kids to avoid avoid losing a third of their inheritance to tax. The question is what should you be doing now to minimize taxes to enhance your family's wealth while sustaining your own income?

12 - What's the NIIT? And Why You Need to Care

When President Obama signed the "Affordable Care Act", aka Obamacare, it came with a pretty significant tax bite called the Net Investment Income Tax (NIIT).

From the IRS:
"The NIIT applies at a rate of 3.8% to certain net investment income of individuals, estates and trusts that have income above the statutory threshold amounts."

3. What individuals are subject to the Net Investment Income Tax?

Individuals will owe the tax if they have Net Investment Income and also have modified adjusted gross income over the following thresholds:

Filing Status	Threshold Amount
Married filing jointly	$250,000
Married filing separately	$125,000
Single	$200,000
Head of household (with qualifying person)	$200,000
Qualifying widow(er) with dependent child	$250,000

Taxpayers should be aware that these threshold amounts are not indexed for inflation.

If you are an individual who is exempt from Medicare taxes, you still may be subject to the Net Investment Income Tax if you have Net Investment Income and also have modified adjusted gross income over the applicable thresholds.

Now, you may be thinking, "I don't have anywhere near that $250,000 in MAGI to worry about this tax. So, what's the big deal?"

See where it says: *"Taxpayers should be aware that these threshold amounts are **not indexed for inflation**"?* (Emphasis mine).

Not indexed for inflation... Hmmmm..where have we heard that before? Oh yeah, the provisional income rules for the taxation of Social Security benefits as well as the Alternative Minimum Tax.

When the legislation to tax Social Security and then the Alternative Minimum Tax were first enacted very few people were affected, thus no outrage, as only "the rich" paid. Now almost everyone pays some tax on their Social Security benefits. (As of the 2017 tax bill fewer taxpayers are caught in the AMT web, thankfully.)

Pretty sneaky, eh? Oh, but it gets worse. How is Net Investment Income derived? Again, straight from the IRS website:

What are some common types of income that are not Net Investment Income?

*Wages, unemployment compensation; operating income from a nonpassive business, Social Security Benefits, alimony, tax-exempt interest, self-employment income, Alaska Permanent Fund Dividends (see Rev. Rul. 90-56, 1990-2 CB 102) and **distributions from certain Qualified Plans (those described in sections 401(a), 403(a), 403(b), 408, 408A or 457(b)).** (emphasis mine)*

Here the IRS is telling us that distributions from retirement accounts are NOT subject to the NIIT, which is factually correct. What they don't say is that distributions from retirement accounts are counted as income to <u>determine</u> if you need to pay the NIIT on your dividends, interest and capital gains. Some might even call this an error of omission. I certainly do.

Let me give you an example of how this works.

You are single. You have $180k income. You take a $50k IRA distribution. Your total income now is $230k. That $50k IRA distribution is not subject to NIIT. But if you have capital gains, interest and dividend income, those will be subject to the NIIT because that $50k IRA distribution put you above the $200k threshold!

Large distributions from your qualified accounts could add 3.8% to your tax rate on dividends, interest and capital gains. That is nearly a 25% tax increase!

Yeah, I get it. This tax won't affect many people so it's not a huge deal. Well, it's not a big deal now but I assure you it will be because of inflation, just like taxes on Social Security.

So, what do you do to avoid this??? Take a guess…

Distributions from the Roth are not counted in your Adjusted Gross Income and thus will not ensnare you in NIIT trap.

Once again, YAY for the ROTH! Is there anything it can't do?

13 - How to Keep the Governor Out Of Your Pocket

If you live in one of the nine states in the US with no income tax you are free to skip this section. However, you may want to read on for a couple reasons:

1. If they incorporate an income tax at some point in your state. (I'm looking at you Washington state!)
2. You move to a state that has an income tax. For instance you move 50 miles south from Chattanooga to Georgia.

The rest of us will be faced with *potentially* paying income taxes on our IRA distributions. Now, be advised, many states have income deductions and exemptions for retirees that working stiffs don't get. So, even if the state has an income tax, you still may not pay any.

Take Georgia for instance. If you're over 64 years old, you pay NO tax on your Social Security income and you pay no tax on the first $65k of retirement income distributions, per person. Essentially, even though there is a rather high state income tax, Georgia retirees can have a lot of income before they pay any state tax.

However, not all states are like that. Take Massachusetts where all IRA distributions are taxed at 5.15% as of this writing (July 2018).

Thus, if you're a resident of Massachusetts and have a $50,000 IRA distribution, you're going to pay $2,500 to the state and another $11,000 to the Feds if you are in the 22% bracket.

A $50,000 IRA distribution in Massachusetts nets you only $36,500!

Now if you had the Roth...well, well. That $50k distribution would net $50k spending money.

Some states are more favorable than Massachusetts. Some are less so. It's up to you to figure that out. You actually might be surprised which states are tax favorable.

I have a video series on the state-by-state taxes for retirees plus my top eight states for retirees to live. Just go to www.youtube.com/heritagewealthplanning

Don't just assume the states with no income tax are the most tax friendly. Believe it or not, Kentucky is ranked more tax-friendly than neighboring Tennessee for retirees even though Kentucky has a state income tax and Tennessee doesn't.

Of course, if you have a Roth income tax won't matter. Because a Roth is...

...you got it, tax free!

14 - Even Jeff Bezos Should Have a Roth 401k

Another benefit of the Roth is one many overlook. This is the ability to fund a Roth 401k regardless of your income. High income earners, even millionaires, can fund a Roth 401k if their plan offers it.

I know many of you are reading this and saying "Josh, you've really lost it now. Why on earth would a high-income earner want to fund a Roth with after-tax money when she is in a high tax bracket?"

To which I say "Even after reading this far in this book you still doubt the power of the Roth?"

First, let me explain the basics of a 401k plan. There are three parts:
1. Elective deferrals
2. Employer contributions
3. Profit sharing

Elective deferrals are the money you choose to forgo from your paycheck in order for it to go into your retirement account. You have one of two choices for where to put this money, the tax-deferred, i.e., the Traditional 401k or the tax free, the Roth 401k.

The money you contribute to the Traditional side *reduces* your taxable income in that year by the amount you deferred (see chapter 7). Whereas Roth contributions do not reduce your current income.

The second part of your 401k plan is the employer contributions. Employer contributions go *entirely* to the Traditional side even if you put your own money into the Roth side. You don't pay any tax on the employer contributions until you make a withdrawal from the account.

Finally, your 401k consists of the profit sharing contribution your employer may offer. These contributions, if any are made, also go into the Traditional side of the ledger.

Some firms have significant profit-sharing contributions, many have nothing. So, don't get too caught up on this. But if your firm does offer a decent profit sharing contribution on top of an employer match you may see the tax-deferred side grow quite large.

Given every penny of your employer contributions goes to the pre-tax side, I find this to be an incentive to put your own money into the Roth because of future tax hedging strategies.
If you have assets in the tax free (Roth) side and assets in the tax-deferred (Traditional) side, you have more flexibility in how to deal with future tax laws.

Situations change folks. The best way to deal with changing times is to be nimble and also not have all your eggs in one basket. Everyone knows diversification of investments makes sense, well, diversification of tax strategies does too.

Let's say your salary is $100,000. But you elect to defer $15,000 of that salary into the Traditional 401k. Thus your taxable salary this year is $85,000.

When you reach the age of 70.5 you will be required to take a portion of that $15,000, and whatever growth you have, as taxable distributions. Again, you're only deferring the tax until a later date, you haven't eliminated it.

If, instead of deferring that $15,000, you funded your Roth 401k you'll pay tax on the entire $100,000 salary you earned that year. But that $15,000 and whatever growth it earns will never be taxed again.

Is it worth it? Here's a table to show you how much that extra $15,000 of income will cost you in taxes in the year you contribute to the Roth 401k.

Tax Bracket	Tax on $15,000
10%	$1,500
12%	$1,800
22%	$3,300
24%	$3,600
32%	$4,800
35%	$5,250
37%	$5,550

Table 29

As you can see, if you are in the 37% bracket you will need to decide if it is worth it to pay an extra $5,550 now to avoid any taxes in the future to yourself, your spouse and ultimately your kids and grandkids?

You know where I stand on this. With ALL the other taxes that can be avoided due to you having a Roth as opposed to a Traditional account, the Roth just makes sense, even if it you feel a short-term pain of $5,550.

15 - How Your Teen Can Take Advantage of the Tax Code

I cannot tell you how many times I've been asked this question: "Josh, my 16 year old son has a part time job this summer. Can he open a Roth?"

Yes, he can start a Roth and certainly should. A great strategy is to give him the money to open the account based on the income he made.

Incentivize your children to work by opening a Roth for them

For instance, say he made $5,000 washing dishes over the summer but he wants to spend some of that money. Can't blame him. That's why he worked, to get some spending money. A way to reward him without just handing him over cash is to say, "I'm proud of you getting this job, son. Look at all your peers just lounging around. For your efforts, I'm going to put the amount you made as income into a Roth IRA in your name." And you then send a check for $5,000 to his Roth IRA provider.

Maybe that's too much of a gift for him and doesn't incentivize him to save any of his own money? Then simply match the money he puts into his Roth with your own contribution.

Match what your kid contributes to a Roth

Say he made $5,000 but only wants to put $2,500 in the Roth. Tell him you will match his contributions dollar for dollar up to his income limits. In this case, he gets $2,500 of his own money to spend as he likes, he contributes $2,500 to his Roth and you match it. Now he has $5,000 in his Roth and $2,500 to spend. Not a bad deal in the least.

By the way, there is absolutely nothing wrong with doing this from the IRS perspective. Your son made $5,000 as earned income. As long as no more than $5,000 goes into his Roth he's good to go. Your $2,500 contribution is not a taxable event either. No gift tax to pay, no transfer tax, no income tax or anything. Easy as pie, nothing to report.

Hopefully, your son will continue to do this each year so by the time he graduates college he'll have a nice sum of money saved up in his Roth.

Have Your Working Children File a Tax Return!

The standard deduction of $12k(for those under the age of 65) is much higher than most kids' earnings. So, no tax is owed. But have him file a tax return anyway because his employer most likely withheld income tax from his paycheck. As long as his standard deduction is higher than his taxable income he will get the income tax that was withheld returned.

He will not get back this FICA taxes, mind you. But there are benefits to his reporting income even if it is only $5,000 each year from a Social Security/Medicare perspective. Every $1,375 your child earns is 1 quarter earned towards the 40 they need for full benefits when he retires. Yeah, this may not seem like much now but it could prove huge in the future. (I've done a ton of

videos on this topic on my Youtube channel.
www.youtube.com/heritagewealthplanning).

What if all he did was mow lawns and had no actual paycheck?

He can STILL open a Roth, as long as he reports his income on a 1099. You're going to want to research this a bit to make sure he pays his FICA taxes. It's really not that hard. Just a couple simple forms and VOILA! He can contribute to his Roth.

How about my daughter who babysits?
She will have the exact same scenario as the son who mows lawns.

I'm a dentist can I hire my kids to sit in the chair for a marketing picture?

Yes, you can… but, I do urge caution here. Is it *truly* earned income when your kids are just being used for a marketing piece? That's a tough one. However, if you validate they are cleaning up around the office, taking out the trash, scrubbing toilets, etc. and *then* you put them on the payroll, by all means do so! If it's legitimate, absolutely take advantage of what is allowed.

I always advise clients that it's never worth the risk if there is any way an IRS agent could perceive what you're doing is not on the up and up. After all, we're only talking, at most, $5k a year into a Roth. Is it worth it to risk the wrath of the IRS to put $5k into a Roth for a child? I don't think so.

16 - This Is The Worst There Is?

Let's just say I've been able to convince you to go the route of the Roth. You understand the reasons why the Roth is superior, and you decide to take advantage. But, as I've stated before, situations can change. And now you need the money. So what do you do? Simply call up your Roth provider and say, "Send me a check!"

The worst thing that will happen is you will owe taxes and a 10% penalty *on the gains*. That's it. No taxes, no penalties on your principal, i.e., contributions, just on the gains.

For all the benefits of the Roth to have this as the worst-case scenario makes it even more of a slam dunk. You may wonder what the worst-case scenario with a Traditional IRA is? Taxes and a 10% penalty on the *entire* amount.

Even in the worst-case scenario, the Roth outshines.

BONUS SECTION - A Few Bones for the Disbelievers

It's not always peaches and cream when it comes to the Roth, mind you. There are a couple things you need to consider before you drink the Kool Aid completely.

Bonus 1 - Roth's Are Included in Estate Tax Calculations

Roth IRAs are included in your estate for estate tax purposes. Yes, the vast majority of Americans will die without owing any federal estate tax. But if you are one of the couple thousand Americans who have an estate over $20 million at the time of this writing (2018), your Roth will be included.

Now, with that said, everything you own will be included; Your Traditional IRA, life insurance, home, etc. A Roth is not unique. But it's important to know that while a Roth is income tax free it's not estate tax free.

"Ahhh, that's no big deal Josh, we don't have anywhere near $20 million." I get it. You may not be that wealthy. But do you live in MA? NY? MN? PA? OR? All of these states, and a host more, have state estate tax and/or inheritance tax.

Roth IRAs will be part of the calculation to determine how much your estate owes in taxes to your state when you pass on. Massachusetts, for instance, taxes your estate if it is greater than $1million. Not hard to get to that threshold in MA with property values so high. Have a decent sized life insurance policy and a house? Guess what??? In MA, you have a taxable estate!

If you have a Roth, it will be taxed as part of that estate. Just be advised.

Bonus 2 - Roth's Are Subject to Creditors of NON-SPOUSE Beneficiaries

As of a 2014 Supreme Court ruling, ALL non-spouse inherited IRAs are subject to creditors.

So, if you die and leave your IRA to a child who decides to open up a pizza shop and the pizza shop fails, his creditors will seek reprieve in what was *your* IRA, Roth or Traditional.

You may want to consider other options to simply leaving your retirement accounts outright to a child or grandchild if you feel there is a risk of a lawsuit.

Say your children are surgeons using risky yet cutting-edge procedures. Their malpractice premiums are through the roof. Why is that? Because they get sued all the time!

Plaintiffs will look to every asset your child owns for payment, including the Roth you left him or her.

Bonus 3 - Roth's Do Not Get a Step-Up in Basis

This one is huge. And again, it not only applies to the Roth but to ALL tax-deferred accounts including annuities.

Let me explain what the Step-Up Basis means.

You buy a stock for $100 today. In ten years that stock is worth $1,000 and you get hit by that bus driver, again. When you die, the executor of your estate will capture the Date of Death (DOD) valuation of all your accounts on the day of your death.

In this case, this stock was worth $1,000 on your DOD.

The person you left the stock to could then sell it for $1,000 and pay no tax. That $900 gain escapes taxation. This is a huge benefit of the tax code that many taxpayers do not take advantage of.

Now, be advised, the step up in basis rules applies to any property you own outside a retirement/annuity account. A house, an investment property, a collectible item, *anything* you own that has grown in value above your initial cost will receive the step up in basis. To reiterate, this means your beneficiary's basis is the value of that asset on the day you die.

It's very easy to identify date of death valuations for investment accounts. Simply find out how many shares were owned and the price per share on your day of death. But what if the property is something that has no daily trade volume and price? In this case, your executor will want to engage an appraiser to determine the value. It's very important to get appraisals done on all property where a value cannot easily be determined simply due to the potential tax consequence.

Okay, but what does this have to do with the Roth IRA? Well, a couple things.

First, because a Roth has no step-up basis and transfers completely tax free to the heir without going through probate the Roth is an easy account for a beneficiary to liquidate while waiting on the remainder of the estate to be settled.

The heir may say, "boy, I could really use $50,000 to pay off that credit card debt I've accumulated. I could wait until dad's estate finally settles in 9 months and sell the house or just cash out the Roth now. After all, it already transferred to me. And I won't owe ANY taxes on it!"

What do you think that heir may do? Wait until the estate settles??? Maybe, maybe not.

Sometimes the best thing we can do for long term growth of accounts is to put restrictions on when the account can be distributed. Annuities are famous for having huge surrender charges in the first few years of the account. Believe it or not, these penalties may actual help the annuity owner by giving a reason *not* to touch the money.

IRAs work the same way. You get hit with a sizeable penalty if you take a distribution out before you are 59.5. Because of the penalties many people will look for alternative cash sources before tapping their IRA or annuity. However, one who inherits an IRA, be it a Traditional or Roth, will not face any early distribution penalties. Thus the pain to take that money out is minimized for the heir to cash in the IRA you left.

Secondly, because the Roth does have mandatory distribution requirements for non-spouse beneficiaries, some heirs may think it's just easier to liquidate the whole thing in order not to be bothered by RMDs. I've seen this happen quite a bit actually.

Lastly, a decedent may have the bulk of his or her assets in real estate which is providing a decent income stream as well. The heir might be inclined to say "Why would I sell the property, with all the costs associated with listing it, when I can continue to get an income stream from it? I'll just go ahead and liquidate that Roth to give me the quick influx of cash I could use."

Actually, that may be a good move. In some regard the Roth IRA may be negatively impacted because of it being easily transferable and tax free to heirs.

Bonus 4 - Roth Distributions May Impact Financial Aid

Lastly, and this can *easily* be overlooked by those who are considering college for a youngster, distributions from a Roth are included in many colleges financial aid calculations.

Again, this negative is not exclusive to the Roth. All retirement plan distributions negatively affect financial aid. But it's important to recognize that being tax free does not mean there are not consequences in other areas.

"A tax-free return of contributions is reported as untaxed income on the Free Application for federal Student Aid (FAFSA) and other financial aid application forms (such as the CSS/Financial Aid PROFILE form). Untaxed income is added to AGI to yield total income. As much as half of total income will increase the expected family contribution (EFC)." (emphasis mine)
https://www.edvisors.com/education-tax-benefits/retirement-savings/roth-ira/

Doesn't seem right, getting your own money back is income? Crazy, I know. But it is reality when it comes to financial aid and you have to understand that distributions from a Roth could have negative consequences.

I actually like a strategy the folks at Edvisors say when it comes to using your Roth for college funding:

"(One) approach is to wait until after the student graduates and to use the tax-free return of contributions then to pay down student loan debt."

If you are going for financial aid keep your Roth "hidden". The asset itself shouldn't cause any issue on your financial aid application. It is the *distribution* from that asset that is the problem.

Let the child get student loans and *then,* when the student will no longer apply for financial aid, use your Roth to pay off those student loans.

Conclusion

My intent on writing this book was to share with you my love of the Roth IRA. I hope you now have some love for the Roth too. In fact, I hope you love it so much you'll go forth and take action to enhance your own financial life by incorporating the Roth IRA into your plans.

Remember, the Roth doesn't just benefit you, it also provides *huge* benefits to your spouse, your kids and grandkids. Why? Because one of the biggest obstacles you have to financial success is the one overlooked the most; taxes.

Taxes, my friends, are your enemy. Doesn't mean you evade them. You can't do that. But you can minimize them, legally, and the Roth IRA is the perfect tool to do just that.

To learn more, please go to my website at www.heritagewealthplanning.com. Or go to my youtube channel at www.youtube.com/heritagewealthplanning. I have tons of videos, articles, tutorials even courses to help you engage in your financial planning preparedness.

If you want to talk about how to incorporate the Roth into your own plans feel free to contact me at: josh@heritagewealthplanning.com

Blessings,

Josh

About the Author

Josh Scandlen is a CERTIFIED FINANCIAL PLANNER Practitioner and holds a Master's of Science degree in Personal Financial Planning. Josh has provided financial advice to clients since 1998.

Over those 2 decades he has learned that successful financial planning does not need to be complex. He follows the tried and true rule he learned in the Army, "Keep It Simple, Stupid."

Josh used the GI Bill to earn his degree in economics from George Mason University in Fairfax, VA, where he received a number of academic scholarships. He was an instructor for the Virginia Commonwealth University CFP certification program in 2006 and was named as one of "America's Top Financial Planners" by the Consumers Research Council of America for 2008 and 2010.

He served as an infantryman in the U.S. Army's 10th Mountain Division and the Virginia National Guard.

Josh greatly values spending time with his wife and four children. Being raised on a small island in Casco Bay, Maine, Josh is a passionate fan of college and professional hockey and tries to catch a Boston Bruins game at least once a year with his family.

Reach out to Josh at his www.heritagewealthplanning.com